Best Start

MUSIC LESSONS BOOK 2

for
Recorder
Fife
Flute

by Sarah Broughton Stalbow

First published in 2019 by Best Start Publishing

© Sarah Broughton Stalbow, 2019

ISBN: 978-0-6484270-7-0

The moral rights of the author have been asserted.

All rights reserved. Except as permitted under the Australian Copyright Act 1968 (for example, a fair dealing for the purposes of study, research, criticism or review), no part of this book may be reproduced, stored in a retrieval system, communicated or transmitted in any form or by any means without prior written permission.

All inquiries should be made to the author.

All musical compositions by Sarah Broughton Stalbow, except for the following by Dominic G. Harvey: Lesson 10: *Brubeck Eski* and *Jammin'*.

Cover art and text design by Sarah Broughton Stalbow, editing by Rob Stalbow.

A catalogue record for this book is available from the National Library of Australia

Best Start Publishing
www.beststartmusic.com

For teachers and parents

Best Start Music Lessons Book 2 follows on from Book 1 and the material follows a similar format. Each lesson comprises familiar components which build on the skills developed in Book 1.

Teachers can choose the order in which to complete each component or activity. Students may complete a whole lesson in one week, or over multiple weeks, depending on the age and skill of each student. All of the songs can be played on recorder, fife, flute, or Nuvo instruments such as the Toot, allowing students to revisit the material on multiple instruments.

There is a companion book for teachers which includes piano accompaniments for all songs and aural work. Backing tracks for songs and aural work can also be found on the Best Start Music Lessons website: www.beststartmusic.com.

The Best Start Music Approach

Best Start Music Lessons introduce foundational musical concepts and skills to the young beginner. As well as developing musical skills and competencies, these lessons aim to foster a love of music and music making.

Originally developed for children aged 4 to 7 years, it is also a great resource for older students who may progress through the books faster, while still developing a strong musical foundation.

The methodologies of **Kodaly**, **Orff** and **Dalcroze** have provided inspiration for many of the activities in this book, however, Best Start Music Lessons do not claim to embody any one or all of these methods. Inspiration has also been drawn from the works of respected author, educator and composer, **Paul Harris**, and from the wonderful piano classes at the **Australian Music Schools**, Sydney. A list of further reading is provided on the Best Start Music website: www.beststartmusic.com.

The Best Start Music Framework

Principle →	Develops →	Outcomes
Engagement	Enjoyment / Enthusiasm for learning / Motivation	Knowledge
Exposure and varied musical experiences	Musical awareness / Knowledge / Creativity	
Routine	Familiarity / Learning Strategies / Motivation	+ Skills
Build musical knowledge and correct technique	Musical understanding / Literacy / Mastery	
Small manageable steps	Confidence / Enjoyment / Secure learning / Motivation	+ Confidence
Creativity	Enjoyment / Enthusiasm / Application / Motivation	+ Positive sense of self
Repetition	Consolidates learning / Mastery / Independence	
Build effective practice habits	Mastery / Independence	

Solfege note names are used for some singing activities to expose children to another way of naming notes and thinking about sounds.

Kodaly rhythm names are used throughout, rather than western rhythmic notation names. This gives young beginners the ability to easily identify rhythmic values and patterns, and learn to sight read rhythms quickly and accurately.

Music teachers can choose to introduce western rhythmic notation names concurrently, or at a later stage.

Best Start Music Lessons aim to empower children by giving them the tools and skills to decode and analyse music easily.

For Students

This is your book! You can write in it, draw in it, colour it in…

Look out for these symbols for:

 WRITING activities

 COLOURING activities

 Listen or play along with the AUDIO TRACK

 Every time you do an activity that has balloons attached to it, you can colour in one balloon. You can do the activities at home or in your lesson.

There are fingering charts that show you which fingers to use to play the notes in this book.

Wiggle your thumbs, then your first fingers, second fingers, third fingers, then little fingers.

STICKERS

There is a sticker chart at the back of this book. Teachers or parents can give you a sticker for good behaviour, good listening and positive attitude.

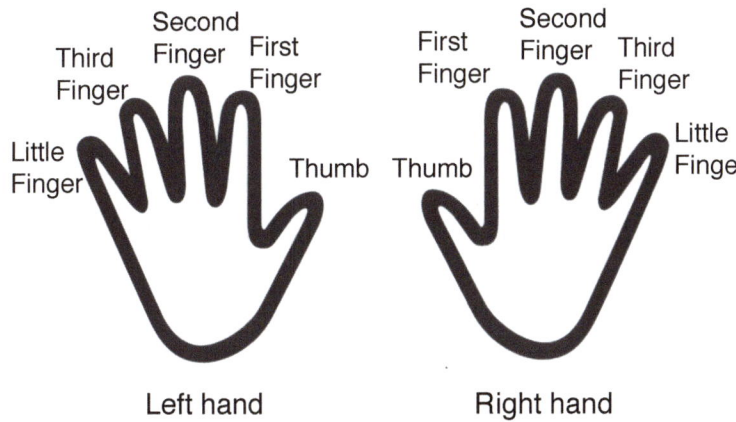

Left hand   Right hand

VERY IMPORTANT!!!

A musical instrument is VALUABLE and BREAKABLE.

Treat yours gently or it will break.

You can find the backing tracks for all of the songs on the Best Start Music Lessons website and YouTube channel: **www.beststartmusic.com**

We really hope you enjoy them as much as we do!

Notes you have already learned

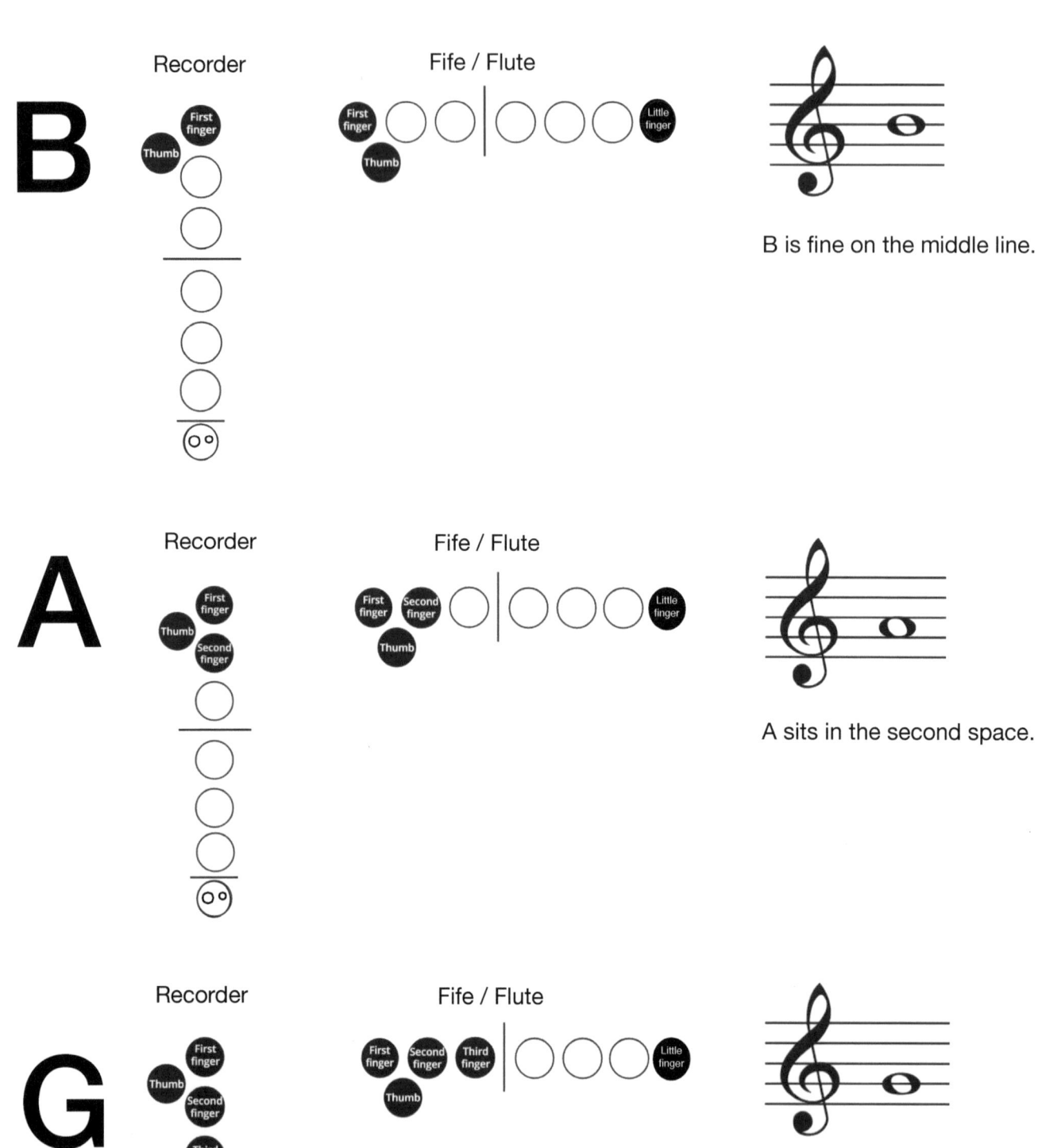

Rhythm

In music RHYTHM is very important. Rhythm is the placement of sounds in time... or how long we hold each note for! When we write music, we have different symbols which show us how long a note should sound for.

There are a few different ways you can name each rhythm symbol.

When you say the RHYTHM NAME it shows you how long the note sounds for.

You may have heard of some of these rhythm names:

Symbol	Rhythm name	Notation name	Value
♩	Ta	Crotchet or Quarter Note	1 beat
♩ (half note)	Ta-a	Minim or Half Note	2 beats
♩. (dotted half)	Ta-a-a	Dotted Minim or Dotted Half Note	3 beats
o	Great Big Whole Note	Semibreve or Whole Note	4 beats
♫	Ti-ti (Tee-tee)	Quavers or Eighth Notes	1/2 a beat each (together make one beat)
♬	Tika-tika	Semiquavers or Sixteenth Notes	1/4 of a beat each (together make one beat)

Lesson 1

1.

Warm Up   Listen to your teacher play some music, the tempo will change between slow and fast.
Listen carefully and clap or walk in time to the music!

2.

Long Notes   Play a B, A, and G for as long as you can with good sound.
Write down how long you held each note for:

Tip: If you are playing the recorder, blow GENTLY…

B _____

A _____

G _____

3.

Tongue   When we start each note with the tip of our tongue, the notes sound clean, clear and professional!

Say: "Too too too too"

Whisper: "Too too too too"

Blow on your hand: "Too too too too"

Blow on your instrument: "Too too too too"

How many notes can you tongue clearly in one breath?

Write your answer here:

4.

Revision   Can you name each of these?

6

5. Rhythm

Say the rhythm names as you clap.

Choose a note to play these rhythms on their own, or as duets.

You could also play these on percussion instruments.

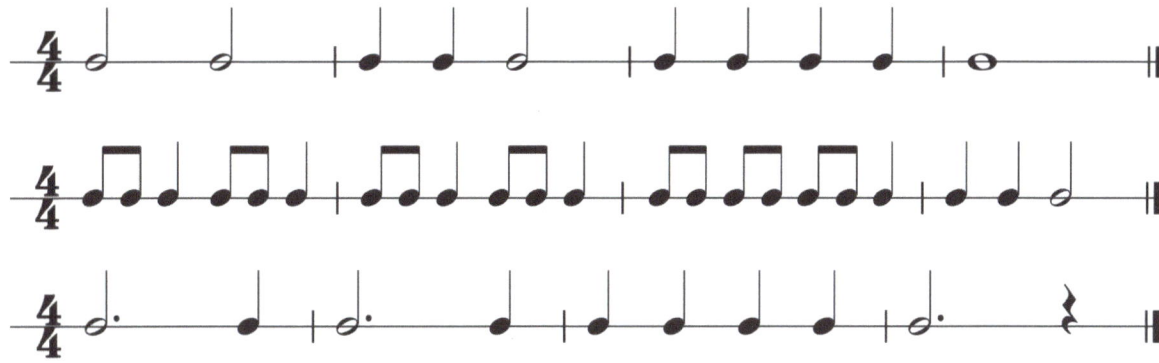

6. Mini Scales

Say: Point to each note and say the note name.

Play: Remember to start every note with your tongue!

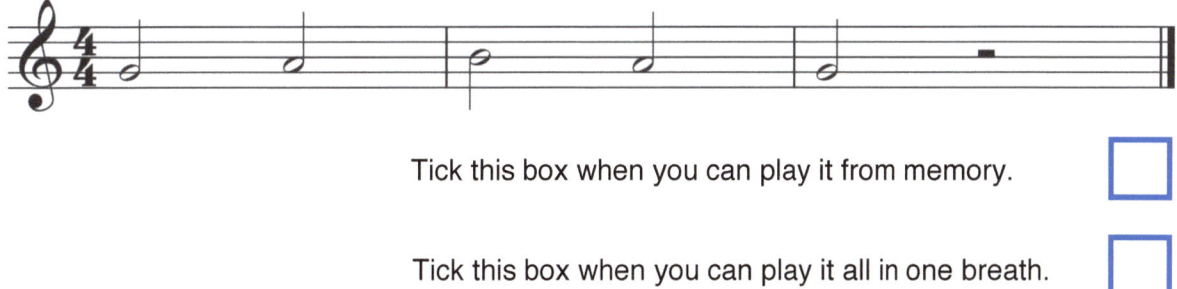

Tick this box when you can play it from memory. ☐

Tick this box when you can play it all in one breath. ☐

7. Read / Write

The PITCH of notes (how high or low a note sounds) is written on the musical STAFF.

The musical STAFF (or STAVE) is made up of 5 lines and 4 spaces.

LINE NOTES look like this: SPACE NOTES look like this:

The line goes right through the middle of the note!   The notes sit between the lines.

Under the notes below, write L for line notes and S for space notes:

7

8.
Aural

Listening: Skipping/Stepping

Listen to some notes or a tune played on any instrument.

1. If the notes STEP smoothly, walk very carefully and smoothly.
2. If the notes SKIP from low to high (or high to low), skip or jump!

Copycats!

Listen and then sing:

    Doh re mi fah soh

    Soh lah soh

    Soh lah ti doh

    Lah soh soh fah mi

    Soh mi doh

Try some more Doh Re Mi patterns!

9.
New Songs

Vámonos! *(Let's go!)* 🎧

Clap Sing Play

First: clap the rhythm.
Next: sing the note names.
Then: play it!

Wait for the 4 bar introduction, then play.

Wait for the instrumental break, then play it again!

10.
New Songs

Icicles 🎧

Remember to Clap Sing Play

Wait for the 4 bar introduction, then play.

11. New Songs

Twilight Lullaby

Remember to Clap Sing Play

Wait for the 4 bar introduction, then play.

Wait for the 4 bar instrumental break.

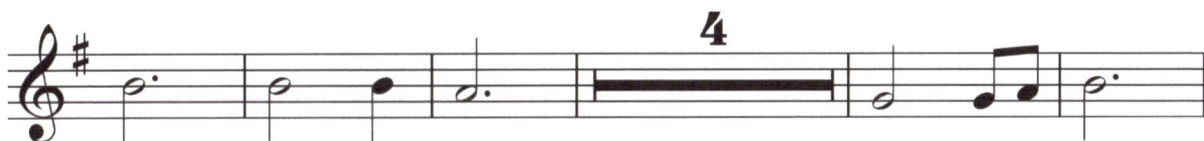

molto rit

12. Listen and Move

Hoedown from Rodeo

by Aaron Copland

Aaron Copland was an American composer and this music is from his ballet "Rodeo", which tells the story of a cowgirl trying to fit in with the men. A hoedown (or barn dance) is part of a rodeo competition in the American West. At a hoedown people do square dancing. Try some square dancing moves to this music! Notice how the music is in groups of 8 beats.

1. Standing in 2 lines facing each other, walk forward 8 steps then back 8 steps.

2. Join hands in a circle, walk to the right 8 steps then to the left 8 steps.

3. Link arms with your partner, skip around each other for 8 beats, then change directions and skip for 8 beats.

4. Do-si-do your partner for 8 beats one way and then the other.

Lesson 2 🔵🟡

1. Warm Up

Partner clapping game:

1. Clap your hands 2 times.
2. Clap hands with your partner 2 times.
3. Repeat.

You can also do this in a circle, clapping hands with the people on either side of you.

Different things to try:

1 clap + 1 partner clap

Different combinations, for example, tap your knees, stomach, clap, partner clap - repeat!

2. Long Notes

Play a B, A, and G for as long as you can with good sound.

Write down how long you held each note for:

B _____

A _____

G _____

Tip: If you are playing the recorder, blow GENTLY…

3. Breathing

Balloon breathing

Posture: Stand straight with both feet flat on the floor.

Imagine your lungs are BALLOONS. When you breathe in, they fill up with air. When you breathe out, they deflate.

1. Put your hands around your lower ribs.

2. Breathe in for four counts, feel your lungs EXPAND (get bigger) as they fill up with air.

3. Breathe out for four counts, feel your lungs DEFLATE (get smaller) as the air goes out.

Look in a mirror and check that your shoulders stay down, and don't creep up to your ears as you breathe in! Try your long notes again after taking a deep, full breath with good posture.

4. Elements of Music

Two beat rest (two beats silence)

SLUR - a curved line that goes over (or under) different notes means to play the notes smoothly in one breath.

Can you play these notes smoothly in one breath?
Imagine you are blowing a long note, and move your finger up and down.

STACCATO - a dot under or over a note means to play it short and detached. Make sure you tongue each note!
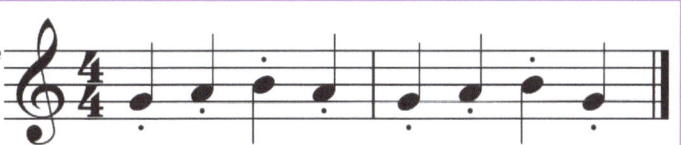

5. Mini Scales

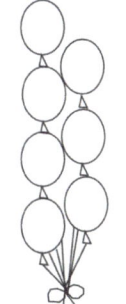

Point to each note and say the note names, then play.

Now SLURRED

Now STACCATO

6. Rhythm

Say the rhythm names as you clap.

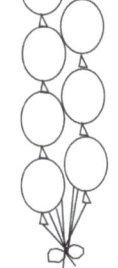

Point to the TIME SIGNATURE - how many beats are in each bar?
Choose a note to play these rhythms on their own, or as duets.

7.

Aural

Echo Game

1. Turn around so you can't see your teacher.
2. Listen to your teacher play a note - it will be either B, A or G.
3. Without looking, find the note on your instrument so that you are echoing your teacher!

Copycats!
Listen and then sing:
- Doh re mi fah soh
- Soh lah soh
- Soh lah soh fah mi
- Mi fah mi re doh
- Soh mi soh
- Soh mi doh

Try some more Doh Re Mi patterns!

8.

New Songs

Groove Machine 🎧

Remember to Clap Sing Play

Wait for the 8 bar introduction.

Point to all of the staccato notes and play them first.

Wait for an 8 bar instrumental break.

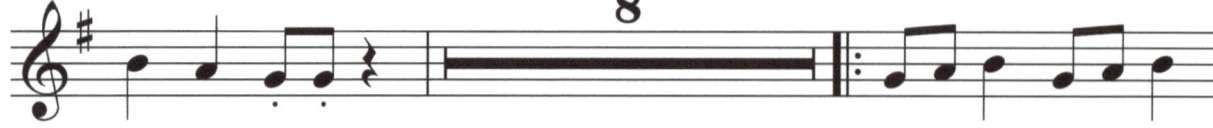

Don't forget the repeat!

9. New Song

Gliding 🎧

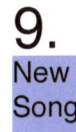

Notice the slurs in this song and play them first.

Remember to Clap Sing Play

Wait for the 8 bar introduction.

This means one whole bar rest.

Wait for the instrumental break, and then play it again.

10. Listen and Move

Waltz No. 2

by Dimitri Shostakovich

Have a go at waltzing - a three step pattern with your feet.

Also try different body percussion combinations in 3/4 time. For example:

| 1 | 2 | 3 | \| 1 | 2 | 3 | \| 1 | 2 | 3 | \| 1 | 2 | 3 |

knees, click, click,   knees, click, click,   knees__(float hands up)   knees_____

11. Read / Write

In music we use the notes A B C D E F G. After G we go back to A again.

You can think of the notes like going up and down stairs.

As you go up the stairs the notes sound HIGHER. As you go down the stairs the notes sound LOWER. Listen to your teacher play them, and point to each note with your finger.

When you go from one note to it's next door neighbour, this is called a STEP. When you jump over a note to get to the next note, this is called a SKIP (or a JUMP).

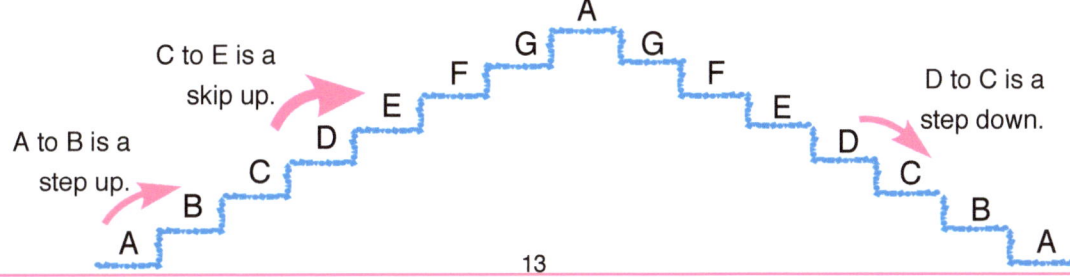

Lesson 3 ●●●

1.
Warm Up

Feet and Hands

1. Keep the beat with your feet: **Ta ta ta ta**
2. Clap **Ta-a** with your hands.
3. Clap **Ti-ti** with your hands.

Keep your feet going at a steady pulse!

Make it harder:

1. Keep the beat with your feet: **Ta ta ta ta**
2. Clap **Ta-a** with your hands.
3. Continue clapping **Ta-a**, but when your teacher says "change", clap **ti-ti.**
4. When your teacher says "change" again, change back to clapping **Ta-a**.

2.
Long Notes

Play a B, A, and G for as long as you can with good sound.

Write down how long you held each note for:

B _____

A _____

G _____

Tip: If you are playing the recorder, blow GENTLY...

3.
New Note

C

Fife / Flute

Recorder

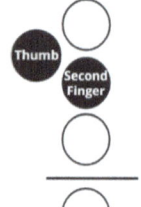

Wobbles!

While you blow a long, smooth stream of air, move your fingers between B and C like this: B C B C B C B C.

Make it harder: wobble between A and C.

Which two fingers move up and down together?

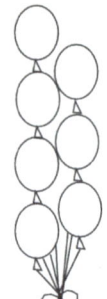

← C is the second space from the top.

4. Mini Scales

Point to each note and say the note names, then play.

Now SLURRED

Now STACCATO

5. Read / Write

Notes that move by STEP go to their next door neighbour - either from a LINE to a SPACE, or from a SPACE to a LINE.

Notes that SKIP (or JUMP), skip or jump over their next door neighbour! You will notice a gap on the staff between these notes.

Write **S** for a step, **J** for a jump, and **R** if the same note is repeated.

6. Aural

Step up or down?

1. Listen to your teacher play two notes.
2. Do they step up or step down?
3. Find two notes on your instrument that step up.
4. Find two notes that step down.

Copycats!

Listen and then sing:
 Doh re mi fah soh soh soh
 Soh lah ti doh
 Doh ti lah soh fah
 Soh mi doh

Try some more Doh Re Mi patterns!

7.
Rhythm — Say the rhythm names as you clap.

Choose a note to play these rhythms on their own, or as duets.
You can also play these on percussion instruments.

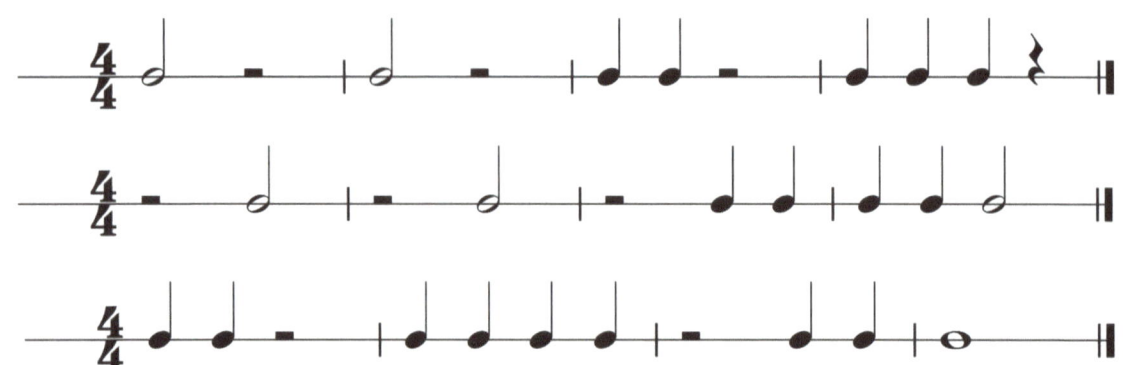

8.
New Songs — **Paradise** 🎧

Remember to Clap Sing Play

Wait for an 8 bar introduction, then play.   Point to the two beat rests.

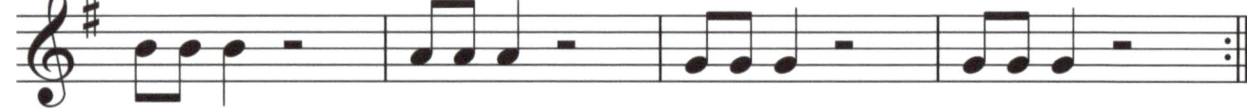

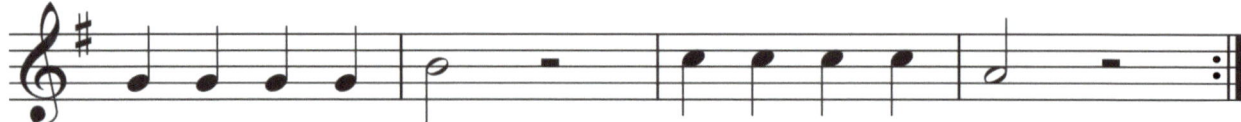

Go back to the beginning and play it all again!
Keep repeating until the music stops.

9. Gently 🎧

New Song

Check the time signature, how many beats are in each bar? You will need to count the rests!

Remember to Clap Sing Play

Wait for an 8 bar introduction, then play.

mp

Fine

This means one whole bar rest.

Wait for the 3 bar instrumental, then go back to the beginning and finish at "Fine" (Italian for "finish"!)

10. Compose

Make up a short song in 3/4 time that you could waltz to.

Try using some slurred notes.

When you've made up a song, write it down so you can perform it again!

17

Lesson 4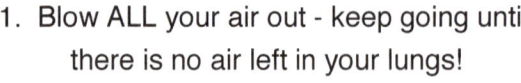

1. Breathing

The "In" Breath

1. Blow ALL your air out - keep going until there is no air left in your lungs!
2. RELAX.
3. Don't *do* anything - just *feel* the air whoosh back into your lungs!

Notice how you don't have to lift your shoulders up or tense your muscles to breathe in.

The "Out" Breath

4. Now let your air out very gradually and slowly to a "sss" sound.
5. Time yourself - how many seconds can you "sss" for?!

Do the same exercise but this time blow very gently, as if you are bending the flame of a candle, not blowing it out!

2. Long Notes

Play a B, A, G and C for as long as you can with good sound.

Write down how long you held each note for:

B _____   G _____

A _____   C _____

Wobbles

While you blow a long note, lift your fingers up and down to change between these notes:

B and C

A and C

G and C

3. Rhythm

Say the rhythm names as you clap.

Two Ti-ti's together looks like this: One on its own looks like this:

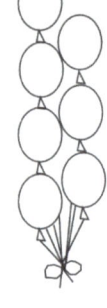

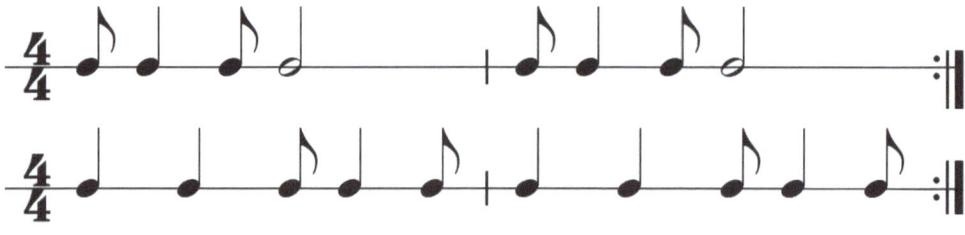

4. Elements of Music

Dynamics

f Forte - loud	mf Mezzo forte - moderately loud	<	Crescendo - gradually getting louder
p Piano - soft	mp Mezzo piano - moderately soft	>	Decrescendo or diminuendo - gradually getting softer

5. Mini Scales

Point to each note and say the note names, then play.

Try some different dynamics. First *forte*, then *piano*, and with a *crescendo* and *decrescendo*.

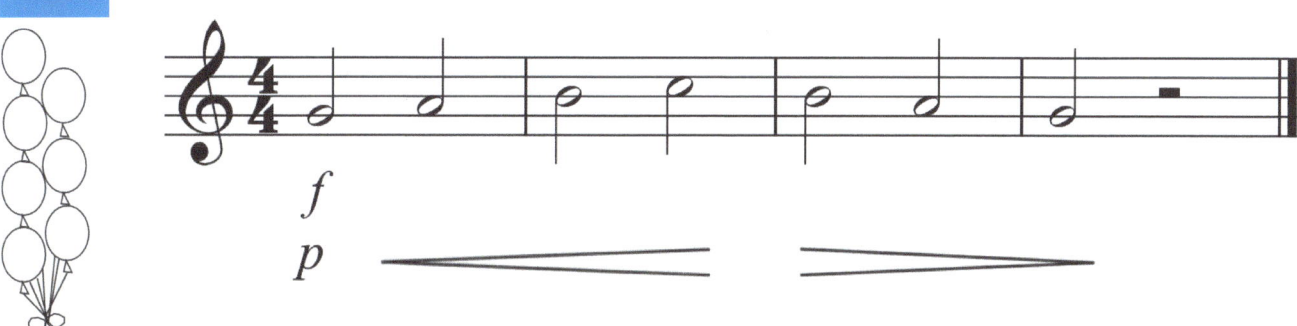

6. Aural

Listening: High/Low

1. Listen to two notes played by your teacher.
2. Sing the notes.
3. Which one sounds higher - the first one or the second? Which is lower?

Copycats!

Listen and then sing:

    Doh re mi fah soh

    Soh mi soh soh soh

    Soh lah soh fah mi

    Mi fah mi re doh

    Doh mi soh soh

    Soh lah ti doh

Try some more Doh Re Mi patterns!

7. New Song

Orange Juice 🎧

Notice the dynamic markings - what do they mean?

Remember to Clap Sing Play

Wait for the 10 bar introduction, then play.

Wait for the 8 bar instrumental break.

8. Compose

Say this short poem out loud:

　　Red, blue, yellow, green.

　　Rainbow in the sky.

　　Orange, pink, purple too,

　　See it way up high.

Make up a tune that uses the rhythm of the words!

9. New Song

The Elephant and the Grasshopper 🎧

Remember to Clap Sing Play

Wait for a 2 bar introduction, then play.

10. Read / Write

The musical staff is like a ladder. Notes at the top of the staff sound higher than notes at the bottom of the satff.

When notes step up, their pitch gets HIGHER. When notes step down their pitch gets LOWER.

Write the direction of each STEP. Write **U** for **UP** and **D** for **DOWN** under each pair of notes.

Write the direction of each SKIP. Write **U** for **UP** and **D** for **DOWN** under each pair of notes.

Remember the musical alphabet is A B C D E F G.
Complete the musical alphabet by writing in the missing letter names:

| A | B | C | | E | | G |

| A | | C | D | | F | |

Lesson 5

1. Warm Up

Name Game

1. Clap a steady beat.
2. Each person take a turn to say their name to the beat.
3. Can you figure out what rhythm names are used to say your name?
4. Try saying your favourite food, favourite colour, what you had for breakfast etc all to a steady beat.
5. You can make up silly sentences, but stay in time with the beat!

2. New Note

E

Fife / Flute

Recorder

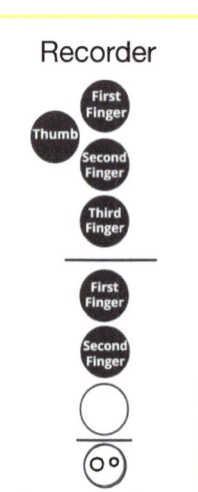

 ← E is the first line.

3. Long Notes

Take a deep, relaxed breath and let your air out slowly until you have no more left.

Write down how many seconds you hold each one for:

B _____   E _____

A _____   C _____

G _____

Wobbles

TWO finger wobbles!

While you blow a long note, lift your fingers up and down together to change between these notes:

C and A

B and G

G and E

4.
Elements of Music

Remember:

Two Ti-ti's together looks like this:

One on its own looks like this:

And as a rest it looks like this:

Half a beat SILENCE.

5.
Rhythm

Say the rhythm names as you clap.

When notes are not on the main beats we say the rhythm is SYNCOPATED.

The third and fourth lines below use some SYNCOPATED rhythms.

6.
Mini Scales

Point to each note and say the note names, then play.

Say the note names and notice the SKIPS from line to line.

This is an ARPEGGIO.

7. New Song — Red Moon 🎧

Remember to Clap Sing Play

Wait for the 3 bar introduction, then play.

mf

(This is the same tune as the beginning!)

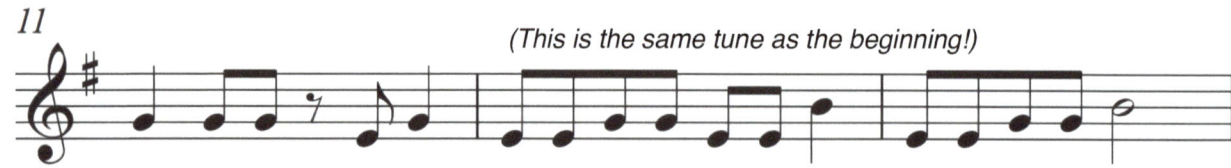

8. Aural

Major / Minor - Happy / Sad

Listen to the chords played on the piano.

If it sounds happy (Major), stand up straight with arms above your head.

If it sounds sad (minor), crouch down low or touch your toes.

Copycats!

Listen and then sing:
- Doh re mi fah soh lah soh
- Soh lah soh fah mi
- Mi soh lah soh
- Soh lah ti soh doh

Try some more Doh Re Mi patterns!

9. New Song

Drifting

Find the STEPS and SKIPS in this song.

Remember to Clap Sing Play

Wait for an 8 bar introduction.

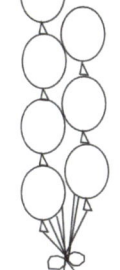

mp

Wait for an 8 bar instrumental break, then play it again!

10. Listen and Move

Listen to these songs and clap the beat.

Notice the SYNCOPATED rhythms.

1. *In the Mood* by Glenn Miller
2. *Take 5* by Dave Brubeck
3. *The Rite of Spring (Sacrificial Dance)* by Igor Stravinsky

11. Read / Write

How long does it take you to say the note names?

Time yourself with a stopwatch and write how many seconds here: _____

Now play the notes and write how many seconds it takes here: _____

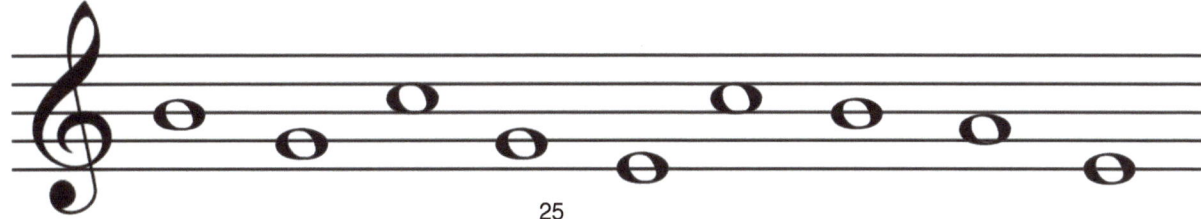

Lesson 6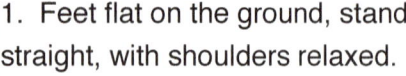

1. Breathing

Posture first.

1. Feet flat on the ground, stand straight, with shoulders relaxed.

2. Breathe in through your mouth and feel your body expand all around.

3. Try placing your hands on your bottom ribs, or just above your belly button to feel your body expand in all directions.

Breathe in and let your air out to "sss" for the number of seconds below. You must make sure that you breathe ALL your air out with each "sss":

Breathe IN	Breathe OUT
4 seconds	4 seconds
4 seconds	6 seconds
3 seconds	7 seconds
2 seconds	4 seconds
2 seconds	6 seconds
1 second	7 seconds

2. Long Notes

Notes: B A G E C

Take a deep, relaxed breath and let your air out slowly until you have no more left.

Write down how many seconds you hold each note for.

Wobbles

TWO finger wobbles!

While you blow a long note, lift your fingers up and down together to change between these notes:

C and A

B and G

G and E

3. Mini Scales

Point to each note and say the note names.

Play ALL SLURRED and then ALL TONGUED.

G mini scale

E mini arpeggio

4. Elements of Music

TIME SIGNATURE

A two on the top means that there are two beats in each bar.

A four on the bottom means that they are **Ta** (crotchet) beats.

5. Rhythm

Say the rhythm names as you clap.

Choose a note to play these rhythms on their own, or as duets.
You can also play these on percussion instruments.

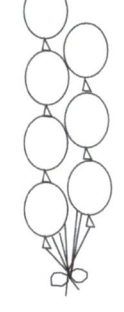

6. New Song

Boot Scootin' Betty

Remember to Clap Sing Play

Wait for a 4 bar introduction.

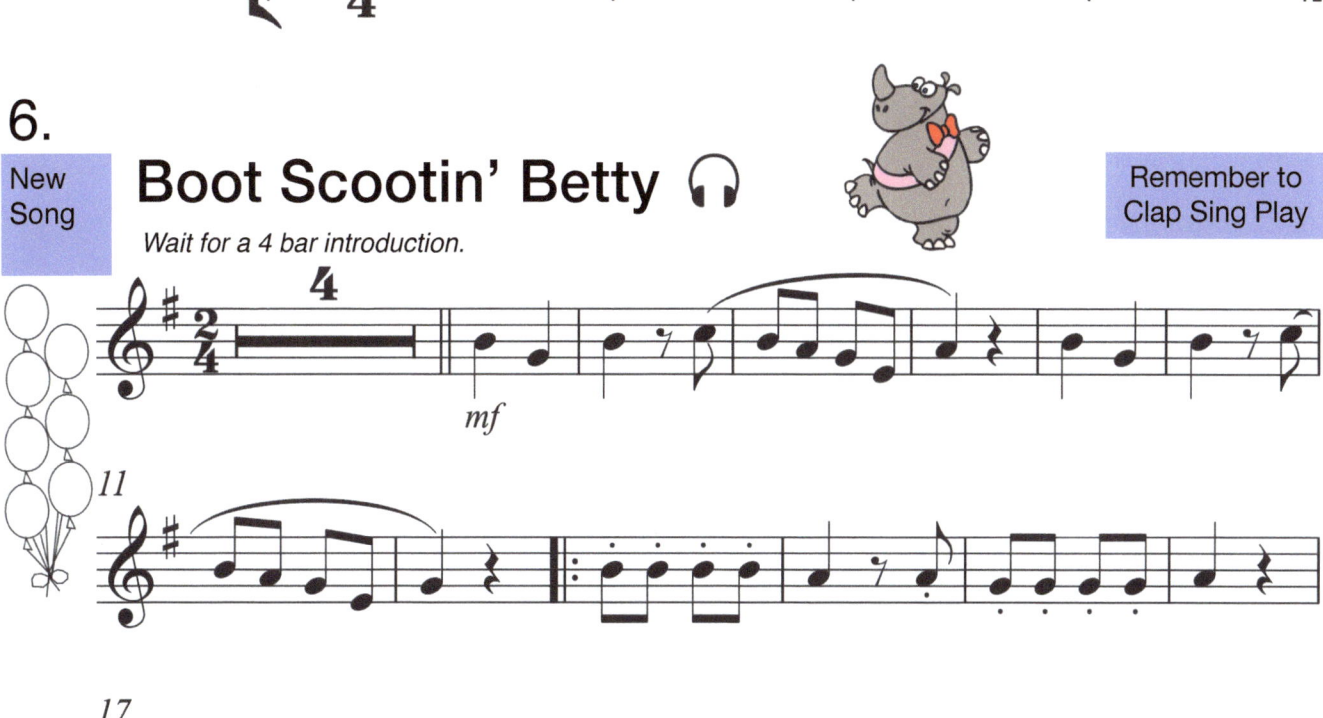

Wait for the 8 bar instrumental break, then play the tune again.

7.

Aural

Triple or Duple?

Swaying music has 3 beats in each bar (triple).

Marching music has 2 beats in each bar (duple).

1. Listen to the music.
2. Is the beat in groups of 3 or 2?
   Is it swaying music or marching music?
3. Sway or march in time with the music!

Copycats!
Listen and then sing:
  Doh re mi fah soh
  Soh lah soh fah mi
  Mi fah soh lah soh
  Soh, fah mi re
  Doh re mi fah soh
  Soh fah mi re doh
Try some more Doh Re Mi patterns!

8.

New Song

My Pet Llama

Remember to Clap Sing Play

Wait for the 4 bar introduction.

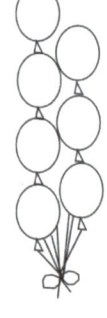

9.
New Song

Calm Chameleon

You can play this as a duet with your teacher.

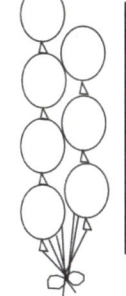

Remember to Clap Sing Play

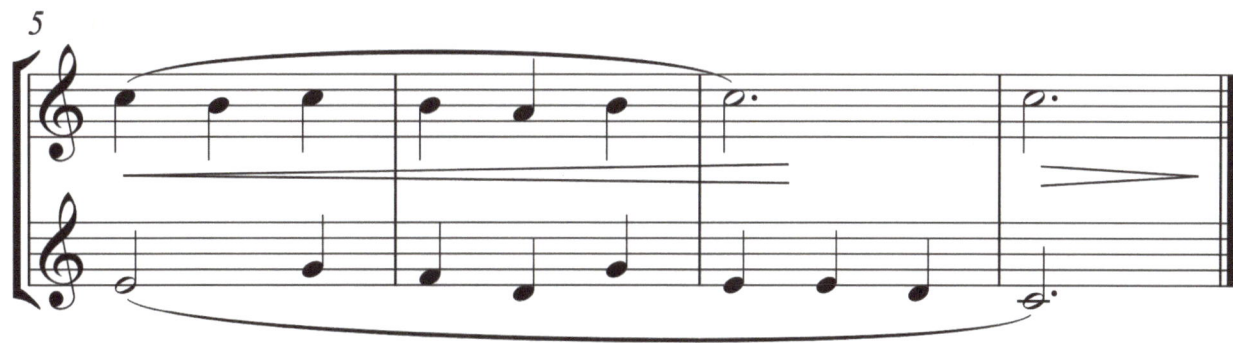

10.
Listen and Move

The Can Can

by Jaques Offenbach

The Can Can is a high energy dance in 2/4 time that originated in France. It involves high kicks, swishing skirts, and often splits and cartwheels. It was originally danced by both men and women, however today it is usually danced by a chorus line of women.

Learn how to do the Can Can!

11.
Read / Write

Draw notes on the staff.

Line notes: E G B

Space notes: A C

Write different rhythms. ➡

Then play the notes!

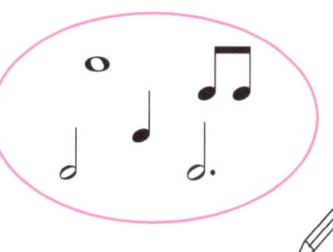

Lesson 7

1. Warm Up

Listen to your teacher play two notes.
Say which one is higher and which one is lower.

2. New Note

F

Fife / Flute

Recorder

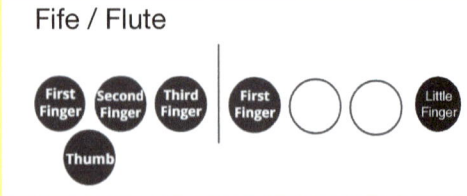

← F is in the first space.

3. Long Notes

Notes: B A G E F C

For each note, take a deep, relaxed breath and let your air out SLOWLY until you have no more air left.

Write down how many seconds you play each note for.

Wobbles

While you blow a long note, lift your fingers up and down together to change between these notes:

F and G

E and F

F and A

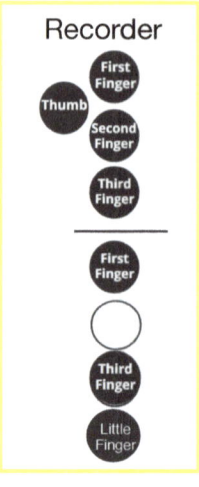

4. Mini Scales

Point to each note and say the note names. Play ALL TONGUED and then ALL SLURRED.

G mini scale

F mini scale

F mini arpeggio

E mini arpeggio

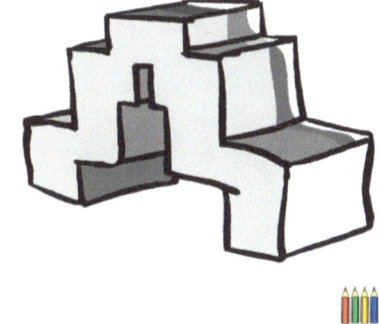

5.

Rhythm Say the rhythm names as you clap.

In the first line notice how two Ti-ti's can be written joined together:

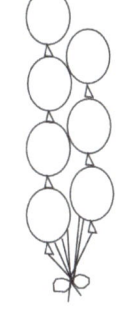

6.

New Song Play this tune. Do you know this song? What is it called?!

Try playing the same tune starting on a **B**. What notes will you use?

When you have played it, write the notes on the blank staff below:

7. New Song — Fossil Fenzy

Wait for a 1 bar introduction.

Remember to Clap Sing Play

mf

8. Aural

Listen - Clap - Sing

Listen carefully to a short melody.

Clap the rhythm back to your teacher.

Listen to the melody again.

Now sing it back!

Hot Cross Buns - Movable Doh

Mi re doh,

Mi re doh,

Doh doh doh doh

Re re re re

Mi re doh.

You can start singing this song on any pitch, give it a go!

9. Read / Write

Reading Music

Music notes are written on 5 lines and 4 spaces - this is called the STAFF or STAVE.

You can remember the notes on the LINES like this:

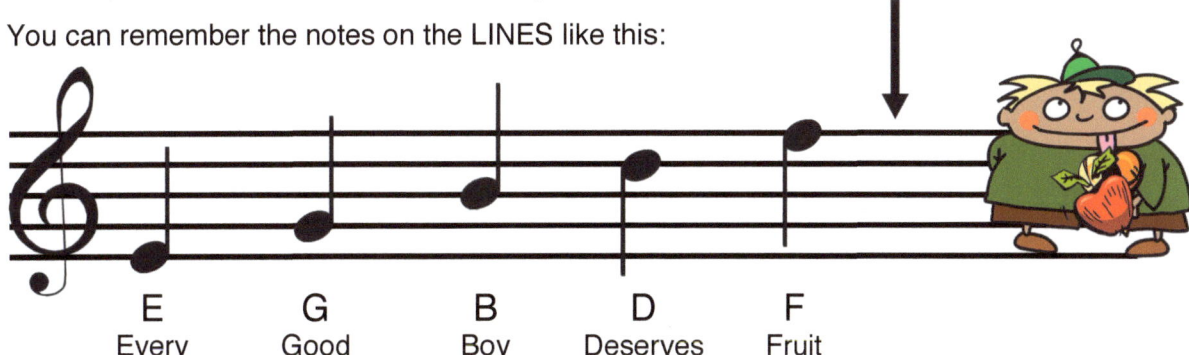

E - Every
G - Good
B - Boy
D - Deserves
F - Fruit

You can remember the notes in the SPACES like this:

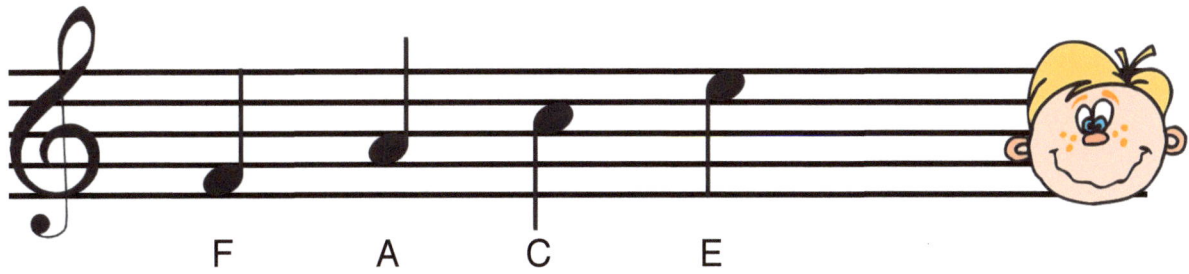

F A C E

Draw notes on the LINES and write their letter names underneath.

Hint: Copy exactly how it is written above!

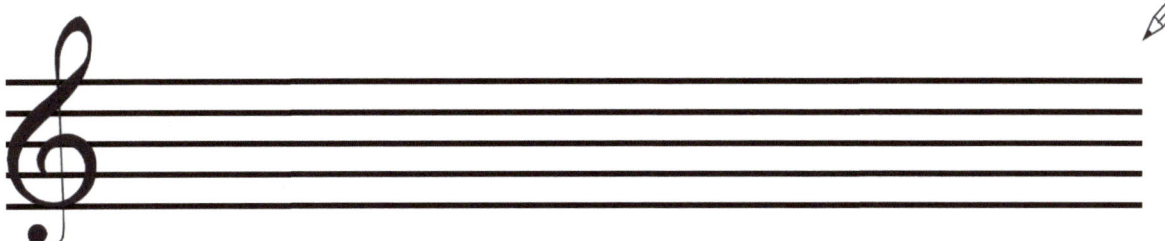

Draw notes in the SPACES and write their letter names underneath.

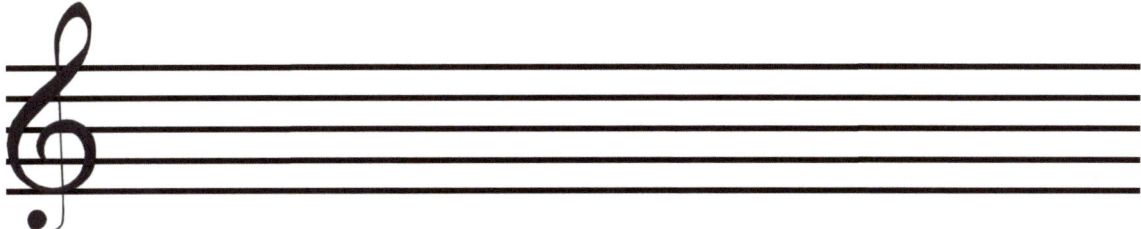

Lesson 8

1. Warm Up

Inner Hearing

1. Count a steady beat out loud eg 1, 2, 3, 4
2. Whisper it, and then just hear it internally.
3. Count silently in your head and choose a beat to play on.
4. Make it harder: everyone choose a different beat to play on!

2. Long Notes

Notes: B A G E F C

For each note, take a deep, relaxed breath and let your air out slowly until you have no more air left.

Write down how many seconds you hold each note for.

Wobbles

TWO finger wobbles!

While you blow a long note, lift your fingers up and down together to change between these notes:

C and A   G and E
B and G   A and F

3. Elements of Music

Tika tika

Four notes in one beat. Each note is worth a quarter of a beat.

TIE A curved line joining notes of the *same* pitch means to hold for the value of *both* notes (don't tongue the second note!)

Hold for: 2   +   1   1 + 1   1 + 1/2

4.
Rhythm — Say the rhythm names as you clap.

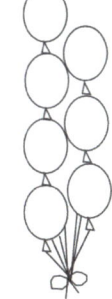

5.
New Song — **Feel the Beat**

Remember to Clap Sing Play

Wait for a 1 bar introduction.   Find the tika-tikas and play them.

6.
Mini Scales

Point to each note and say the note names.

Play ALL TONGUED and then ALL SLURRED.

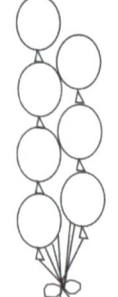

F mini scale

F mini arpeggio

7.
Aural

Learn this song in solfege:

    Doh mi soh soh lah lah soh__

    Doh mi soh soh fah mi re__

    Doh mi soh soh lah lah soh__

    Fah fah mi mi re re doh__

Sing it STACCATO and then LEGATO.

Now sing it starting on a different pitch.

8.
New Song

Walk the Dog

Wait for the 3 bar introduction.

Find the bars with tied notes and play them.

Remember to Clap Sing Play

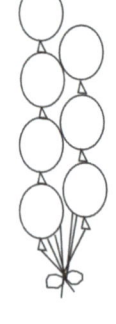

f

p (second time)

7

11

15

f

9.
Compose

Improvise!

Make up a short song called:

"Opposites"

Think about how you can include some musical "opposites".

For example:

p (piano) - f (forte)
crescendo - decrescendo
staccato - legato
high - low
fast - slow
going up - going down

10.
Read / Write

Crack the code!

What words do these notes spell? Write the letter names under the notes.

Solos

Pick one of the songs you have learned and perform it as a solo for your class, your family, pets, or your toys!

Hint:

Remember the rhyme for the LINES is:
Every **G**ood **B**oy **D**eserves **F**ruit.

And, remember the SPACES spell:
F A C E

Lesson 9

1. Breathing

Ho!

1. Feet flat on the ground, stand straight, with shoulders relaxed.
2. Say "Ho"
3. Now take a slow breath in with your mouth in the same shape as when you say "ho", or you can think of inhaling and saying "ho" - a backwards "ho"!

This "backwards ho" allows your throat to open and lets you take in lots of air.

Breathe in and let your air out to "sss" for the number of seconds below. You must make sure that you breathe ALL your air out with each "sss":

Breathe IN	Breathe OUT
4 seconds	4 seconds
4 seconds	6 seconds
3 seconds	7 seconds
2 seconds	4 seconds
2 seconds	6 seconds
1 second	7 seconds

2. New Note

D

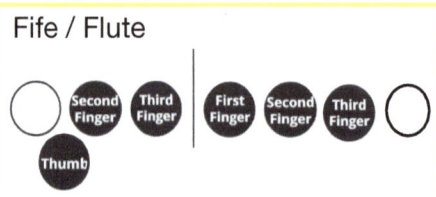

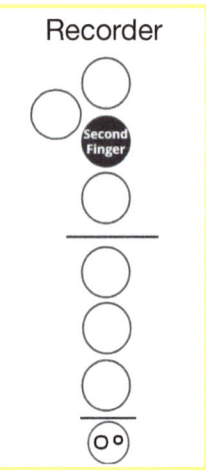

D is drawn around the fourth line.

3. New Song

Good Deeds   Play this song to practise playing D.

4. Mini Scales

Point to each note and say the note names.

Play ALL TONGUED and then ALL SLURRED.

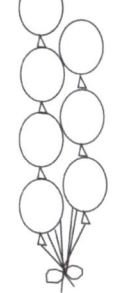

G mini scale

G mini arpeggio

A mini scale

5. Elements of Music

A dot AFTER a note adds on half the value of the original note:

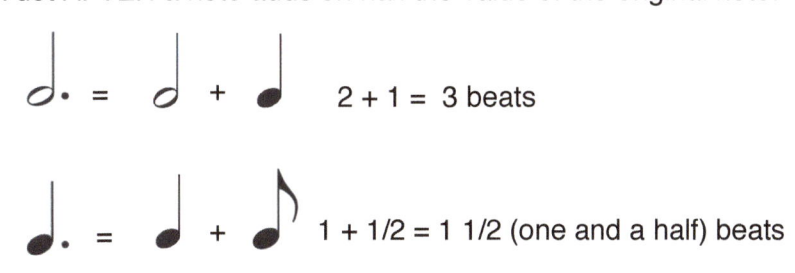

This is a very common rhythm:

Say: Ta - i ti

6. Rhythm

Say the rhythm names as you clap.

39

7.
Aural

Listen - Clap - Sing

1. Listen carefully to a short melody.
2. Clap the rhythm back to your teacher.
3. Listen to the melody again.
4. Now sing it back!

Echo Game

1. Turn around so you can't see your teacher.
2. Listen to your teacher play a note - it can be any note you have learned.
3. Find the note on your instrument so that you are echoing your teacher!

8.
Compose

Choose one person to be the soloist - everyone else is the orchestra.

•. The orchestra makes up a short theme to play together, for example:

G, A, B, C, D, D, D__

- The soloist improvises a short solo.
- The orchestra responds with their theme.

Keep repeating, each time the soloist improvises a different solo and the orchestra answers with their theme.

9.
Read / Write

Have a go at writing the notes for the orchestra theme you composed.

Hint:

B goes around the middle line.

A sits in the second space.

G goes around the second line.

10. Morning Song

New Song

Wait for a 2 bar introduction.

Remember to Clap Sing Play

11. Sunrise

New Song

Wait for 1 bar introduction.

Remember to Clap Sing Play

Lesson 10

1. Warm Up

Rhythm focus

1. Walk on the spot to a steady beat.
2. Your teacher will call out a rhythm value to clap.
3. Keep clapping that rhythm until your teacher calls out the next one to change to.
4. Your feet should keep a steady beat the whole time!

For example:

Walk on the spot to a steady beat.

Clap **Great Big Whole Notes** several times. When your teacher says to change, everyone should start clapping **Ta-a**.

Continue until the next change when everyone claps **Ta**, then **Ti-ti**, and then **Tika-tika**.

2. Long Notes

Notes: B A G E F C D

For each note, take a deep, relaxed breath and let your air out slowly until you have no more air left.

Write down how many seconds you play each note for.

Wobbles

Play a C, then change to a D.

Which fingers move?

Try playing:

C C C C - D D D D

C C C - D D D

C C - D D

C - D - C - D - C - D

3. Rhythm

Say the rhythm names as you clap.

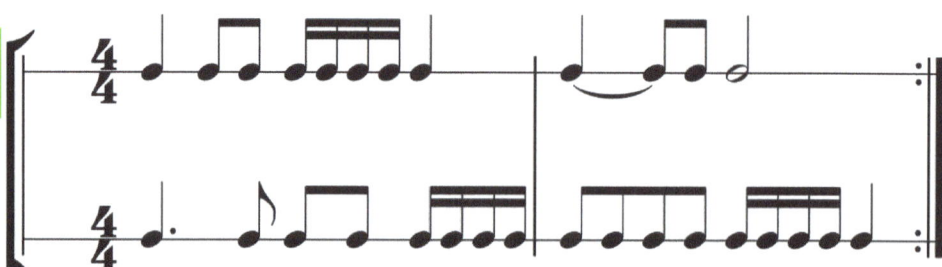

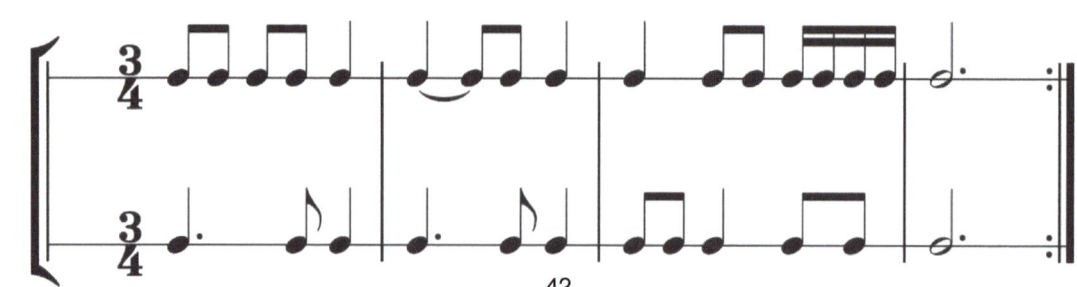

4. Mini Scales

Point to each note and say the note names.
Play ALL TONGUED and then ALL SLURRED.

Tick the boxes when you can play them from memory.

5. Read / Write

Crack the code!    What words do these notes spell?
Write the letter names under the notes.

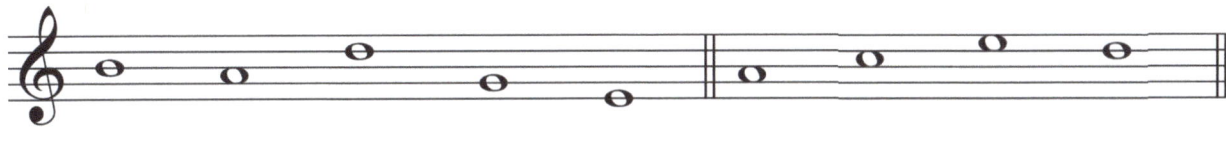

6.

Aural

Twinkle Twinkle in solfege.

    Doh doh soh soh lah lah soh,

    Fah fah mi mi re re doh,

    Soh soh fah fah mi mi re,

    Soh soh fah fah mi mi re,

    Doh doh soh soh lah lah soh,

    Fah fah mi mi re re doh.

Sing it starting on different pitches. You can even try to play it on your instrument!

7.

New Song

Silver Starlight

Remember to Clap Sing Play

You can play this song as a duet with your teacher.

Learn the top part first. When you feel comfortable with the rhythm, learn the bottom part.

9.

New Song

Brubeck Eski

Wait for an 8 bar introduction.

Remember to Clap Sing Play

D G H

Improvise using E, G, A, B and C until the end.

Think of three things you can do now, that you couldn't do when you first started this book? Write them here:

1.

2.

3.

Congratulations!

Stickers

www.ingramcontent.com/pod-product-compliance
Lightning Source LLC
Chambersburg PA
CBHW042141290426
44110CB00002B/74